Contents

Francis Frith: Victorian Pioneer

FRANCIS FRITH, Victorian founder of the world-famous photographic archive, was a complex and multitudinous man. A devout Quaker and a highly successful Victorian businessman, he was both philosophical by nature and pioneering in outlook.

By 1855 Francis Frith had already established a wholesale grocery business in Liverpool, and sold it for the astonishing sum of £200,000, which is the equivalent today of over £15,000,000. Now a very rich man, he was able to indulge his passion for travel. As a child he had pored over travel books written by early explorers, and his fancy and imagination had been stirred by family holidays to the sublime mountain regions of Wales and Scotland. 'What lands of spirit-stirring and enriching scenes and places!' he had written. He was to return to these scenes of grandeur in later years to 'recapture the thousands of vivid and tender memories', but with a different purpose. Now in his thirties, and captivated by the new science of photography, Frith set out on a series of pioneering journeys to the Nile regions that occupied him from 1856 until 1860.

Intrigue and Adventure

He took with him on his travels a specially-designed wicker carriage that acted as both dark-room and sleeping chamber. These far-flung journeys were packed with intrigue and adventure. In his life story, written when he was sixty-three, Frith tells of being held captive by bandits, and of fighting 'an awful midnight battle to the very point of surrender with a deadly pack of hungry, wild dogs'. Sporting flowing Arab costume, Frith arrived at Akaba by camel sixty years before Lawrence, where he encountered 'desert princes and rival sheikhs, blazing with jewel-hilted swords'.

During these extraordinary adventures he was assiduously exploring the desert regions bordering the Nile and patiently recording the antiquities and peoples with his camera. He was the first photographer to venture beyond the sixth cataract. Africa was still the mysterious 'Dark Continent', and Stanley and Livingstone's historic meeting was a decade into the future. The conditions for picture taking confound belief. He laboured for hours in his wicker dark-room in the sweltering heat of the desert, while the volatile chemicals fizzed dangerously in their trays. Often he was forced to work in remote tombs and caves where conditions were cooler. Back in London he exhibited his photographs and was 'rapturously cheered' by members of the Royal Society. His reputation as a photographer was made overnight. An eminent modern historian has likened their impact on the population of the time to that on our own generation of the first photographs taken on the surface of the moon.

Venture of a Life-Time

Characteristically, Frith quickly spotted the opportunity to create a new business as a specialist publisher of photographs. He lived in an era of immense and sometimes violent change. For the poor in the early part of Victoria's reign work was a drudge and the hours long, and people had precious little free time to enjoy themselves. Most had no transport other than a cart or gig at their disposal, and had not travelled far beyond the

boundaries of their own town or village. However, by the 1870s, the railways had threaded their way across the country, and Bank Holidays and half-day Saturdays had been made obligatory by Act of Parliament. All of a sudden the ordinary working man and his family were able to enjoy days out and see a little more of the world.

With characteristic business acumen, Francis Frith foresaw that these new tourists would enjoy having souvenirs to commemorate their days out. In 1860 he married Mary Ann Rosling and set out with the intention of photographing every city, town and village in Britain. For the next thirty years he travelled the country by train and by pony and trap, producing fine photographs of seaside resorts and beauty spots that were keenly bought by millions of Victorians. These prints were painstakingly pasted into family albums and pored over during the dark nights of winter, rekindling precious memories of summer excursions.

The Rise of Frith & Co

Frith's studio was soon supplying retail shops all over the country. To meet the demand he gathered about him a small team of photographers, and published the work of independent artist-photographers of the calibre of Roger Fenton and Francis Bedford. In order to gain some understanding of the scale of Frith's business one only has to look at the catalogue issued by Frith & Co in 1886: it runs to some 670 pages, listing not only many thousands of views of the British Isles but also many photographs of most European countries, and China, Japan, the USA and

Francis Frith's
Victorian Seaside

Photographic Memories

Francis Frith's
Victorian Seaside

Compiled and edited by
Terence Sackett

First published in the United Kingdom in 2000 by
Frith Book Company Ltd

Hardback Edition 2000
ISBN 1-85937-159-0

Paperback Edition 2004
ISBN 1-85937-667-3

British Library Cataloguing in Publication Data

Francis Frith's Victorian Seaside
Compiled and edited by Terence Sackett

Frith Book Company Ltd
Frith's Barn, Teffont,
Salisbury, Wiltshire SP3 5QP
Tel: +44 (0) 1722 716 376
Email: info@francisfrith.co.uk
www.francisfrith.co.uk

Printed and bound in Great Britain

Front Cover: **Felixstowe,** from the beach 1899 44513

The colour-tinting is for illustrative purposes only, and is not intended to be historically accurate

AS WITH ANY HISTORICAL DATABASE THE FRITH ARCHIVE IS CONSTANTLY BEING CORRECTED AND IMPROVED
AND THE PUBLISHERS WOULD WELCOME INFORMATION ON OMISSIONS OR INACCURACIES

1895 a new size of postcard was permitted called the court card, but there was little room for illustration. In 1899, a year after Frith's death, a new card measuring 5.5 x 3.5 inches became the standard format, but it was not until 1902 that the divided back came into being, with address and message on one face and a full-size illustration on the other. Frith & Co were in the vanguard of postcard development, and Frith's sons Eustace and Cyril continued their father's monumental task, expanding the number of views offered to the public and recording more and more places in Britain, as the coasts and countryside were opened up to mass travel.

Francis Frith died in 1898 at his villa in Cannes, his great project still growing. The archive he created continued in business for another seventy years. By 1970 it contained over a third of a million pictures of 7,000 cities, towns and villages. The massive photographic record Frith has left to us stands as a living monument to a special and very remarkable man.

Canada – note the sample page shown above from the hand-written Frith & Co ledgers detailing pictures taken. By 1890 Frith had created the greatest specialist photographic publishing company in the world, with over 2,000 outlets – more than the combined number that Boots and W H Smith have today! The picture on the right shows the Frith & Co display board at Ingleton in the Yorkshire Dales (left of window). Beautifully constructed with a mahogany frame and gilt inserts, it could display up to a dozen local scenes.

Postcard Bonanza

The ever-popular holiday postcard we know today took many years to develop. In 1870 the Post Office issued the first plain cards, with a pre-printed stamp on one face. In 1894 they allowed other publishers' cards to be sent through the mail with an attached adhesive halfpenny stamp. Demand grew rapidly, and in

Frith's Archive: A Unique Legacy

FRANCIS FRITH'S legacy to us today is of immense significance and value, for the magnificent archive of evocative photographs he created provides a unique record of change in 7,000 cities, towns and villages throughout Britain over a century and more. Frith and his fellow studio photographers revisited locations many times down the years to update their views, compiling for us an enthralling and colourful pageant of British life and character.

We tend to think of Frith's sepia views of Britain as nostalgic, for most of us use them to conjure up memories of places in our own lives with which we have family associations. It often makes us forget that to Francis Frith they were records of daily life as it was actually being lived in the cities, towns and villages of his day. The Victorian age was one of great and often bewildering change for ordinary people, and though the pictures evoke an impression of slower times, life was as busy and hectic as it is today.

We are fortunate that Frith was a photographer of the people, dedicated to recording the minutiae of everyday life. For it is this sheer wealth of visual data, the painstaking chronicle of changes in dress, transport, street layouts, buildings, housing, engineering and landscape that captivates us so much today. His remarkable images offer us a powerful link with the past and with the lives of our ancestors.

Today's Technology

Computers have now made it possible for Frith's many thousands of images to be accessed almost instantly. In the Frith archive today, each photograph is carefully 'digitised' then stored on a CD Rom. Frith archivists can locate a single photograph amongst thousands within seconds. Views can be catalogued and sorted under a variety of categories of place and content to the immediate benefit of researchers.

Inexpensive reference prints can be created for them at the touch of a mouse button, and a wide range of books and other printed materials assembled and published for a wider, more general readership. The day-to-day workings of the archive are very different from how they were in Francis Frith's time: imagine the herculean task of sorting through eleven tons of glass negatives as Frith had to do to locate a particular sequence of pictures! Yet the archive still prides itself on maintaining the same high

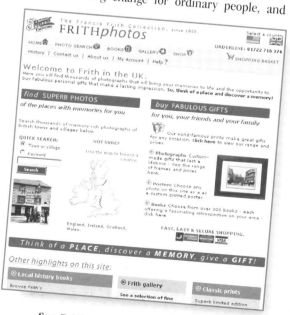

See Frith at www.francisfrith.co.uk

standards of excellence laid down by Francis Frith, including the painstaking cataloguing and indexing of every view.

It is curious to reflect on how the internet now allows researchers in America and elsewhere greater instant access to the archive than Frith himself ever enjoyed. Many thousands of individual views can be called up on screen within seconds on one of the Frith internet sites, enabling people living continents away to revisit the streets of their ancestral home town, or view places in Britain where they have enjoyed holidays. Many overseas researchers welcome the chance to view special theme selections, such as transport, sports, costume and ancient monuments.

We are certain that Francis Frith would have heartily approved of these modern developments in imaging techniques, for he himself was always working at the very limits of Victorian photographic technology.

The Value of the Archive Today

Because of the benefits brought by the computer, Frith's images are increasingly studied by social historians, by researchers into genealogy and ancestory, by architects, town planners, and by teachers and schoolchildren involved in local history projects.

In addition, the archive offers every one of us an opportunity to examine the places where we and our families have lived and worked down the years. Highly successful in Frith's own era, the archive is now, a century and more on, entering a new phase of popularity.

The Past in Tune with the Future

Historians consider the Francis Frith Collection to be of prime national importance. It is the only archive of its kind remaining in private ownership and has been valued at a million pounds. However, this figure is now rapidly increasing as digital technology enables more and more people around the world to enjoy its benefits.

Francis Frith's archive is now housed in an historic timber barn in the beautiful village of Teffont in Wiltshire. Its founder would not recognize the archive office as it is today. In place of the many thousands of dusty boxes containing glass plate negatives and an all-pervading odour of photographic chemicals, there are now ranks of computer screens. He would be amazed to watch his images travelling round the world at unimaginable speeds through network and internet lines.

The archive's future is both bright and exciting. Francis Frith, with his unshakeable belief in making photographs available to the greatest number of people, would undoubtedly approve of what is being done today with his lifetime's work. His photographs, depicting our shared past, are now bringing pleasure and enlightenment to millions around the world a century and more after his death.

The Victorian Seaside
An Introduction

'We love our haunts by the sea; the poorest among us regards his favourite resort pretty much as the rich man does his country seat... How the eyes brighten at the sight of a familiar spot! And how vividly the old assocuations crowd back to the mind - memories of glowing careless days, that gave new life to the jaded worker, and caused the brain-weary to forget their ineffable tedium vitae.' (1895)

The text accompanying these photographs is extracted from a late Victorian tourist guidebook to the seaside resorts of Britain. It is therefore genuine and offers a true picture of the preoccupations and attitudes of its period. Resorts and individual features are thus referred to in the present tense, and the original spelling and punctuation have been retained for the purposes of authenticity. The introductory paragraph quoted reveals all the hallmarks of Victorian popular journalism – it is more than a little sentimental and overblown, yet it made a direct appeal to the romantic spirit that dwelt within even the most humble and workaday Victorian, such as Mr Pooter, Grossmith's hero of 'Diary of a Nobody'.

Some of the photographs in 'Francis Frith's Victorian Seaside' were included in the original Victorian guidebook, for the Frith archive was one of the most significant of its period, and its images were much sought after by publishers. To us the photographs conjure up memories of the archetypal old-fashioned family holiday most of us remember from our childhoods. The nature of our own impressions might mislead us into thinking that the pictures were similarly nostalgic to the Victorian reader. However, they showed the British holiday at its most modern and desirable. The resorts depicted are the equivalent of those shown in the glossy colour holiday brochures of today. These Victorian photographs, therefore, were showing reality, the world as it was, and not the world as we recall it through our modern nostalgia.

The Victorian commentaries themselves are hardly nostalgic, for like a modern guidebook they offer sensible and practical advice to visitors. They describe the type of holiday they might

expect from each resort - the quality of the beach, whether it was sand or shingle, how safe was the bathing, whether children were well catered for, what walks there were in the neighbourhood and what local beauty spots were to be recommended.

For us, the buildings we see in the photographs are imbued with nostalgia; we cannot help viewing them as period architecture. Yet at the time the photographs were taken, in many of the buildings the mortar had barely dried. Time and again the Victorian writer tells of local councils and joint-stock companies embarking on radical development along the seafronts, and building lodging-houses, hotels, dining-rooms and a plethora of places of amusement.

We must remember that just half a century earlier most of the resorts shown in this book barely existed. Previously there had been just a few fishermen's huts and an empty sea front where a few hardy travellers whiled away the hours and took rooms at the local inn. Close to the turn of the 20th century, the Victorian writer still refers to them by the sedate title of 'watering-places'.

The seaside resort that we recognise and relish was an essentially Victorian creation, made possible by the introduction of the Bank Holiday Act in 1871 and the creation of the national railway network. Before this time the working man rarely travelled out of his own parish during the course of his life-time. He had little opportunity to. In the polluted cities men and women worked long hours in appalling conditions. Away from the factories life in their cramped tenements was in general colourless and unremitting.

Then suddenly the railways arrived, and the annual Bank Holiday. Trains were now able to whisk the Victorian family a hundred miles away in a few hours to Brighton or Southend, where they could experience an environment that must have seemed like some conjured-up paradise. Imagine the scene at the seaside station when the Victorian working man and his family stepped off the train and arrived on the seafront for the first time: they would have marvelled at the sheer span of horizon, the broad spaces of sea and air, the sparkle of the waters, the extravagance of the architecture including the elegant and exotic pier, the broad stretches of golden sand, the clear, sharp 'ozone'. Imagine, too, the unaccustomed joys of the humble lodging-house: here, there was someone who actually took care of their daily interests, the cooking, cleaning and making of beds.

The commentaries reveal the intense competition between resorts for clientele. Some made no bones about appealing to the common man, and boasted of the various cheap attractions and entertainments to lure the train loads: the music-hall, donkeys, swings, coconut shies, and bathing machines. Such resorts are spoken euphemistically of as 'less pretentious' or possessing a 'joviality unrestrained by any false pride'.

Other resorts made every effort to be more select, laying emphasis on the small number of select hotels, the peace and quiet, and how a happy medium had been achieved between 'excessive gaiety and sheer dullness'. Some holiday towns worked much harder to achieve success, and local councils and businessmen collaborated in the creation of more durable and respectable attractions for the sophisticated and discerning visitor: promenades, terraces, public gardens, marine drives, theatres and pavilions; and, of course, broad stretches of empty sand, 'smooth as velvet', where 'charmingly-dressed ladies' enjoyed sketching and other worthy pastimes.

The words and pictures in this book inevitably recall an age that is long since gone. Yet they bring us a strong reminder, in our age of the ever more exotic, foreign holiday, of the simple and diverse pleasures that the old-style British resort offered to many generations of tourists. Today we may choose to travel to distant continents rather than take our holidays in our own country, but it is hoped that this book will help bring back happy memories of the British seaside resort in its heyday, that so many of us enjoyed.

Redcar

Visitors are unanimous in praise of the fine air, broad sands, and picturesque cliffs and ravines. This little town lies a few miles south from the mouth of the Tees. A sea wall has been constructed, forming a fine terrace 30 feet wide, and there are two promenade piers. The sands of Redcar can nowhere be surpassed in extent, being ten miles in length and a mile broad at low water. They have been characterized as 'smooth as velvet, yet so firm that neither horse nor man leave their imprint on them as they tread the strand'. Redcar consists mainly of one long street, with the backs of the houses on one side turned to the sea. As a watering-place, Redcar dates from 1842, since when it has progressed at quite an extraordinary rate, and certainly owes much to its magnificent sweep of sands. The Durham coast extends opposite, and the mouth of the Tees on one side and the hills towards Saltburn on the other form the boundaries of this delightful watering-place.

Main picture: *Redcar, The Sands 1886* 18133
Below: *Redcar, From the Pier 1896* 37593
Far left: *Redcar, The Esplanade 1886* 18131

Scarborough

This has been called 'the Queen of English watering-places'. Spread out like an amphitheatre upon a bay and promontory, its houses rise tier behind tier away from the sea. The season here lasts from May to October, and during the greater part of this time the fashionable South Cliff, with its terraces, walks, and handsome music-hall, is crowded with pleasure-seekers from all parts of the kingdom. The bathing at Scarborough is famous. Uncontaminated by any large river, the open bay provides water of the greatest purity, transparency, and saltness; the sand is clear, firm and smooth. The scene on the sands on a fine morning is extremely animated. While some visitors are gambolling among the waves, others are riding along the sands on donkeys or horses. Charmingly-dressed ladies may be seen sitting on the rocks, reading, sketching, or engaged in ostensibly useful 'work'; the old castle, the pier and harbour, the brick houses of the old town, and the handsome range of buildings on the cliff forming a beautiful background to the view.

Main picture: *Scarborough, From the Esplanade 1890* 23457
Below: *Scarborough, Foreshore Road 1890* 23464
Top right: *Scarborough, Belmont 1890* 23476

Filey, The Sands 1901 48020a

Filey, The Brigg 1890 23488

Filey

This prosperous watering-place was little more than thirty years ago an insignificant fishing village. Its picturesque position on the cliffs of one of the noblest bays on the east coast of England, and its fine beach, along with its splendid hotels and handsome private houses, make Filey one of the most attractive resorts in the United Kingdom. It is a place of great antiquity - a fact established in 1857, when heavy floods washed away large portions of the cliff, exposing remains of undoubted Roman work. Filey Brigg, the southern boundary of the bay, is a remarkable ridge of rocks, projecting north half a mile into the sea, and perfectly dry at low water. Lashed and beaten by the storms of ages, it presents an appearance of rugged grandeur. The ever-restless waters by day and night beat themselves into a creamy foam against the jagged sides, until the sea itself is hidden beneath the boiling mass, and the air filled with fleecy flakes

Filey, The Promenade 1897 39343

driven hither and thither like unto a December snowstorm. The sea has scooped out large basins which the receding tide leaves full of water, and the visitor may enjoy a delicious bath in these.

Bridlington, The Esplanade and Bandstand 1886 18224

Bridlington

Often called Burlington, the town is pleasantly situated on a gentle acclivity about a mile from Bridlington quay, which lies in the recess of a beautiful bay. It consists chiefly of one long, irregular street with a number of good houses and shops. Bridlington Quay is one of the less pretentious neighbours of Scarborough, sharing its advantages of situation and climate, but without its rather expensive gaieties. The sands are all that family parties can desire. To the north, Bridlington is protected by Flamborough Head, the lion of the neighbourhood, whose airy heights are accessible by an hour's walk or by regular conveyances. The sea-wall promenade, with a pavilion in the centre, extends northward from the harbour a distance of about 700 feet. The wall, including the promenade, was erected between 1866 and 1869, at a cost of £20,000.

Bridlington, The Quay 1893 32050

Skegness

Skegness, The Sands 1899 44197

The flat coast of Lincolnshire is not very well off for watering-places. Skegness sprung up into considerable note since the extension of the railway in 1873. The great attraction is the firm wide sands, on which donkeys, swings, cocoanut-shies, and other amusements for excursionists will be found in full activity during the season. There is an iron promenade pier with pavilion. Dancing and concerts take place in another pavilion in the Pleasure Gardens. From the sand hills along the shore there are extensive views over the German Ocean. Fine sunsets may be watched hence. The curious optical illusion known as the mirage is often seen here to perfection during fine weather, when the sea has the appearance of a sheet of glass. During the dark nights of summer, the phosphorescence of the sea is a very charming sight. At such times, as one walks along the shore by the side of the receding tide, each footprint glows with phosphorescent light.

Hunstanton

On the north-west angle of the coast of Norfolk stands the pretty watering-place of Hunstanton St Edmunds, which, during the summer months, is crowded with visitors, the rooms, which out of the season can be got for five shillings fetching a guinea a week, or more. This latter fact is not surprising when we consider that the little town is perched upon a hill 60 feet or 80 feet above the sea-level, the top of which is a chalk down; the western side forms a picturesque sea-cliff, overlooking a pleasant and safe beach which extends far seaward at low water. It is the only watering-place on the east coast of England with a western aspect, and it commands extensive views of the opposite coast of Lincoln, 20 miles across. On a clear day the noble tower of Boston church may be plainly discerned.

Main picture:
Hunstanton, The Green 1901 47641
Below:
Hunstanton, The Green and Parade 1893 32264

Cromer

F ast stretching out to the east and west of the church that forms such a prominent landmark, Cromer stands high and bracing on its breezy cliffs, from which stairs and zig-zag paths lead down to the sands, which seem to be more and more crowded every summer. It is fortified with an esplanade and breakwaters behind which it holds gallantly out; yet its exposed position is shown by the new lighthouse being built on an eminence a little way back from the shore. On undeveloped tastes Cromer would be thrown away. The cliffs are brown and sandy, the sea blue and the landscape of a universal green. Once up here you can wander for miles along the cliffs in peace and quiet, amongst farms and cornfields, and such a variety of wild flowers as is rarely seen collected together. All these make the cliffs of Cromer a veritable flower garden, and impart a unique and beautiful aspect to this resort.

Main picture:
Cromer, From the Sands 1899 44482
Below:
Cromer, The Lighthouse 1894 33325
Top right:
Cromer, The Sands 1899 44485

Gorleston, The Beach 1894 33392

Gorleston

The pleasant suburb of Southtown and the picturesque village of Gorleston, connected with a tramway with Yarmouth, offer a retreat to those who may find life at the roystering Norfolk watering-place a little too exhilarating - like its air. Much of the country round about is flat and dull. Cyclists, however, might be inclined to give it a high certificate of merit; and there are one or two objects of interest within an easy walk, such as the ruins of Caistor Castle and the Roman remains at Burgh. The great attraction of this neighbourhood is, of course, the Broads, for the sake of which one can forgive many monotonous stretches of reclaimed marsh.

Gorleston, The Harbour 1894 33393

Great Yarmouth

Great Yarmouth, The Promenade and Beach 1894 33386

This is the most important town and port on the East Anglian coast; it is situated at the mouth of the Yare. Briefly, its attractions include firm and extensive sands for bathers, a marine parade, three piers, the Theatre Royal, and an aquarium. The older part of the town adjoins the river, and contains numerous picturesque 'Rows' or lanes, scarcely more than from 3 to 6 feet wide. As Dickens puts it, 'Great Yarmouth is one vast gridiron, of which the bars are represented by the 'Rows''. Some of the best shops are to be found in this quarter, which almost suggests the stifling bazaars of an Eastern city. There is a marine drive, three miles long; and the climax of the Yarmouth saturnalia is reached with the Regatta in August, when the town seems filled with what one may term the concentrated essence of Bank Holiday. Although it styles itself Great Yarmouth to distinguish it from that small Yarmouth in the Isle of Wight, the usual associations of the Norfolk watering-place are less with greatness than with bigness, boisterousness, and a joviality unrestrained by any false pride.

Main picture:
*Great Yarmouth,
The Beach 1899*
44496

Above:
*Great Yarmouth,
The Beach 1887*
19860

Lowestoft

In more ways than one Lowestoft and Yarmouth have long been rivals. They took opposite sides in the Civil War; they each aspired to be the chief seat of the herring fishery; and now they are found eagerly competing for the patronage of summer visitors. Lowestoft is a more select resort; and there is no place on the coast of East Anglia that has more claims on the favour of strangers who seek an invigorating air, a pleasant neighbourhood, and an abundant means of amusement without too much noise and crowd. The harbour, almost entirely reconstructed, is protected by two piers, with a lighthouse showing a red light all night long at the end of each. 'I shall always look upon Lowestoft', says Mr Clement Scott, 'as the very pink of propriety. It is certainly the cleanest, neatest, and the most orderly seaside resort at which I have ever cast anchor. There is an air of respectability at the very railway station – no confusion, no touting, no harassing, and no fuss. I do not think I ever saw so neat a place out of Holland'.

Main picture: *Lowestoft, The Pier Reading Room 1896* 37937
Below: *Lowestoft, The Beach 1887* 19886
Above: *Lowestoft, The Pier from the Sands 1896* 37936

Felixstowe, From the Beach 1899 44513

Felixstowe

With a southern aspect over the estuary of the Orwell, and enough shelter to give it a milder climate than most places on this Suffolk coast, Felixstowe has of late years risen rapidly, and already bids fair to outstrip its old rivals. The visit of the German Imperial Family certainly did much for the place by proclaiming the merits of its sea-bathing; but what has chiefly helped to bring this resort into prominence is the adjacent golf links, now renowned as among the best in England. The single line of the Great Eastern railway to the town was opened in 1877. The summer excursion fares are amazingly low; the courteous officials and fine stations a standing reproach to certain other great railway companies we could mention. As if confidently expecting continued good fortune, Felixstowe has taken plenty of room to grow,

Felixstowe, The Beach 1899 44516a

straggling, as it does, for three or four miles along the bay, from Landguard Fort towards the links.

Southend

Southend, The Pier 1898 41377

This popular resort can be heartily commended to all, but especially to Londoners. It is reached in little more than an hour by the excellent trains of the Great Eastern Railway. It is quite remarkable to see the crowds of Londoners poured into Southend by steamboat and excursion train on a fine summer's day. Passengers to Southend by water are landed on the pier, which many will be surprised to learn is a mile and a quarter in length - the longest in Great Britain. This pier originally cost £42,000, but it was afterwards sold to the always-enterprising Great Eastern Railway Company for £17,000. It was first built of wood in 1838. One may be conveyed right out to sea by the electric tramway, which runs down the pier in five minutes. The coast here is very shallow, and the tide retires nearly a mile from the shore at low water. The old town stretches along the shore eastwards from the pier in a line of shops and small houses inhabited by the boatmen and fishermen, who make up the mass of the population.

Herne Bay

This town dates its history as a watering-place from the year 1830. Extensive speculation in building was followed by failure; but the place has entered on a new lease of life since the advent of the London, Chatham and Dover Railway in 1862. Herne Bay commands a magnificent view over the North Sea. It has excellent sands, and boasts a pier 3,640 feet long, built by Telford in 1832, in addition to a marine parade. The fine clock tower was the gift of a private lady, and cost £4,000. The sea air at Herne Bay is considered to be more bracing than at any other resort in England. Not very long ago people said Herne Bay was too quiet – even dull; we are quite sure the reproach is unjustifiable now, for there has been a great awakening in the town, and it is not too much to say that it will ere long become one of the most popular resorts on the Kentish coast.

Main picture:
Herne Bay, The Esplanade 1897 40158
Below:
Herne Bay, The Parade 1889 22313
Top right:
Herne Bay, The Downs 1894 34054

Westgate-on-Sea

Westgate-on-Sea, The Hotels and Beach 1890 27463

In this fashionable resort we find all the estimable advantages possessed by a place that begins its career as it means to continue. In the past history of Westgate we find no humble fishing village, with its ancient customs and homely cottages; no ill-planned and awkward rights; nothing, in fact, but a lordly soil with lordly owners able to plan and complete a high-class fashionable neighbourhood, much as a great Tottenham Court Road firm of upholsterers would furnish your house throughout. This delightful little watering-place is within the parish of St John's, Margate. As might be expected it abounds in handsome new villas, and is thronged with visitors in summer. It has several splendid hotels, and a railway station of its own. The great reputation for salubrity which this resort has acquired makes it in ideal resort for those pleasure-seekers who long for the very happy medium between excessive gaiety and sheer dullness.

Margate

Margate, The Promenade 1897 39581

Margate's cliffs are bold and picturesque; its sands are broad and firm. Yet 'superior' people think it needful to offer some excuse for their being found at such a place, and are at pains to explain how they must by no means be confounded with the ordinary ruck of Margate's guests. There can be no question as to the past respectability of Margate. The narrow High Street, the old houses hidden away here and there, the shallow harbour – all these show that the town was once a fishing port. There is no affectation, no blasé cynicism about your genuine Margate visitors. Its sands are thronged by a crowd of idlers ready to be easily entertained by jugglers, Punch and Judy shows, and wandering minstrels. There are busy vendors of refreshments and knick-knacks; family parties, encamped with umbrellas and novels; eager children, sprawling babies and their nurses, and scores of adventurous youngsters, wading in the surf or seriously labouring in the sand with spade and wheel-barrow.

Broadstairs

While Ramsgate and Margate are found enacting the traditional comedy of the pot and the kettle – each exclaiming against the vulgarity of the other – it is significant that they seem to join in railing at modest little Broadstairs. This resort, however, needs no defending, having powerful patrons, the most illustrious of whom was Charles Dickens, whose residence at 'Bleak House' is still pointed out as the chief monument of the place the great novelist liked so well. Though Broadstairs has grown somewhat since Dickens's day, it still remains quieter and more select than its larger and noisier neighbours, and is especially in high favour with family parties, who find quite a little paradise on the sheltered beach of 'Our Watering Place'. The Parade is a pleasant walk by the edge of the cliff, which commands charming views of coast and sea and shipping. The sea-front retains much of the honest, old-fashioned simplicity characteristic of Broadstairs.

Main picture: *Broadstairs, The Harbour 1897* 39592
Below: *Broadstairs, from the Cliffs 1897* 39589
Top left: *Broadstairs, The Promenade 1902* 48842

Ramsgate

Ramsgate, The Harbour 1901 48028

From the end of the pier Ramsgate looks very well indeed. The port, astir with boats and shipping, backed by a group of large hotels and handsome shops; the houses picturesquely crowded in the gap in the heights; the cliffs, on either side crowned by fine terraces. At night, too, when the winding, sloping streets light their lamps, and the hotels and cafes around the harbour are alive with visitors, one might almost fancy that one was in a lively foreign seaport, especially as all the world is abroad to take the cool evening air, and the French boatmen are heard chattering in their own tongue. The sands here are not so extensive as at Margate. From the cliffs the view is wide and attractive, reaching over the sandy flats at the mouth of Sandwich Haven, and the Downs, crowded with the shipping of all nations, to Deal and the South Foreland; in fine weather the coast of France can also be discerned. The climate here is considerably milder than that of Margate, having more sun and less wind. Consequently, we find here large numbers of really fine private houses and superior public buildings; nor is this to be wondered at, seeing that the elder Pugin and his son both lived and worked here.

Deal, The Esplanade 1899 44208

Deal

To many people, the principal attraction in this pleasant old Cinque Port will be the ever-changing view of shipping in the Downs. Behind the shelter of the Goodwins, the tourist may enjoy safe sailing by the famous boatmen of Deal. A particularly steep and shingly beach, some three miles in length, affords a capital bathing-ground, duly provided with machines and tents; but caution is necessary in rough weather. In all weathers, however, strangers should look out for the place where the sewage is discharged. There is a stretch of sand at one end where children may disport themselves in safety. The Deal boatmen, limited by statute to the number of fifty-six, are famous for their heroism. Their skill and daring are often put to the proof on this dangerous coast, for beyond the sheltered Channel near the Downs - a vast natural harbour, eight miles long and six miles

Deal, The Esplanade 1899 44206

wide - lie the treacherous Goodwin Sands, from three to seven miles broad, and at low water these are so hard and firm that cricket matches may be played upon them.

Dover

One of the Cinque Ports, Dover is about two hours run from London by express train. During the summer months there is a good service of steamboats between this interesting watering-place and London. The harbour may be divided into three parts, namely: the pent or breakwater, the basin, and the outer harbour. Favourite walks are on the heights to the castle and to Shakespeare's Cliff, which commands a broad view of the shores of France. The castle, as it stands, is practically of the date of Henry II. The summit is crenellated and there are four angular turrets. During the present century the turret was made bomb-proof and was armed with 64-pounder guns. Shakespeare's Cliff is about 350 feet above the level of the sea; its height is supposed to have been greatly diminished by bits of rock falling from its summit. A deep valley separates the cliff from the heights on the other side of the town, which are so arranged as to hold quite a large army, and have spacious and complete barracks.

Main picture: *Dover, The Beach 1890* 25699
Below: *Dover, The Esplanade 1892* 31418

Folkestone. The Leas 1901 48052

Folkestone

Folkestone, The Leas from the Pier 1901 48054

The older portions of the town have steep and narrow streets, but the modern houses on the cliffs are most attractively situated, fronting the well-known promenade called the Leas, from which one may easily reach the beach. The cliff pathway, between this part of Folkestone and Sandgate, is one of the most beautiful walks in the kingdom for lovers of coast scenery. The season here is short and late, and the policy of the townspeople is such as to discourage excursionists and seek the patronage of the higher class of visitors; consequently, the humours of the sands so conspicuous at Margate or at Yarmouth, are hardly to be looked for at Folkestone, where the most exciting pastime is the going and coming of the Channel boats and the landing of their woebegone passengers. There is a lift railway from the Undercliff Gardens to the Leas Promenade on the top of the cliffs.

Hastings

Hastings, The Esplanade 1890 25393

Hastings lies – for the most part – in a hollow, snugly sheltered by hills, except where it slopes southward to the sea. Of course, the increase of houses of visitors must tend to spoil the natural freshness and original individuality of a population, but in Hastings these qualities are preserved to an unusual extent, especially among the fishermen. By the way, the fishing population numbers about 3,000; the trade is extensive and is constantly increasing. Under the East Cliff, 'Dutch' fish auctions are often held. Besides pleasantly laid-out public gardens, Hastings has an admirable park on the steep, turfy slopes of its East and West Hills, which at one point have recently been made more accessible by means of a lift. The bathing here is excellent in every way. Under the Parade near the pier are fine baths, erected on the foreshore in 1879 at a cost of £60,000. The pier is 920 feet long and was built at a cost of £32,000, and has a pavilion capable of seating 2,000 persons. Lord Byron and Charles Lamb have left records of their stay here, the latter describing his sojourn as 'a dreary penance'.

Main picture:
Hastings,
The Lifeboat House
1894 34427

Left:
Hastings,
The Beach 1890 25357

Eastbourne

T o convey any notion at all of this watering-place to those who have never visited it, one must mention that there are noble tree-planted streets and shady avenues, an imposing sea-front of about three miles, an excellent beach of mingled sand and shingle, a pier of the most approved pattern, an abundance of seats and shelters, gardens and promenades, and every convenience for bathing, boating, and fishing, as well as first-class hotels, well-built houses, tempting shops, and irreproachable sanitary arrangements and water supply. The Grand Parade is a beautiful marine treble-terraced walk, which forms an agreeable and fashionable promenade. No one can accuse Eastbourne of being dull nowadays. The centre of public pastimes is Devonshire Park, a sort of miniature Crystal Palace, with a theatre, concert room, cricket and tennis grounds and many other attractions. Illuminated fetes, too, are given here, and it need hardly be said that electric light is not wanting.

Main picture:
Eastbourne, The Parade and Bandstand 1899 43942
Below:
Eastbourne, The Beach 1894 34459

Brighton

Can anyone now realize a Brighton with only 1800 inhabitants, and those mostly poor fishermen? Yet that was the Brighton of little more than a century ago. This famous watering-place owes its present prosperity, in the first place, to a physician, Dr Russell, of Lewes, who removed hence in 1750. He published a treatise on the advantages of sea-bathing, recommending Brighton very strongly. The Aquarium is situated between the Steyne and the Chain Pier, and was erected by a joint stock company at a cost of £130,000 in 1872. We rather think it is more of a promenade than an aquarium, with its elegant corridors, conservatory, and saloons provided with newspapers, periodicals, and the latest telegrams. There are forty-one fish tanks. You can scarcely move on the Parade on a fine afternoon without meeting troops of fair horse-women attended by their riding-masters, sweeping along, perhaps, towards the Downs. The stream of carriages is almost as incessant as on a Drawing Room day at Buckingham Palace. Bands are playing wherever you go, till the very air grows musical.

Main picture:
Brighton, The Beach 1898 41890
Above:
Brighton, The Aquarium 1889 22238
Far left:
Brighton, The West Pier 1894 33717

Brighton, King's Road 1890 27607

Brighton, The Pier 1889 22345

Worthing, The Bandstand 1899 43955

Worthing

Worthing, The Beach 1890 22678

That Worthing has a milder climate than its neighbours is shown by the large quantities of fruit and vegetables which it sends to Covent Garden. Besides being a quiet holiday resort in summer, Worthing is well adapted for delicate persons in winter, when the flourishing lauristinus hedges still brighten its streets. Complaint, however, is made of fogs, and still more strongly of the seaweed, which accumulates on the beach here in such quantities as to become a perfect nuisance. Everyone is aware of the misfortune which befell Worthing, when its water became tainted, and the demon of typhoid descended upon the town. That cloud, however, has now passed away, and the drainage is above reproach. The sands are smooth and hard, and their condition during the summer months has been graphically described as one long mile of nursery. There are many people who prefer this watering-place to Brighton, on the grounds that it is quieter and far more economical to live in.

Bognor Regis

This town is Worthing's twin sister - a quiet, mild, healthy watering-place, situate on a level in the face of the ever-restless Channel. About 1785, Sir Richard Hotham, a wealthy Southwark hatter, who determined upon acquiring the glory of a seaside Romulus, set to work to erect a town of first-class villas in this pleasant spot, with a view to creating a truly recherché watering-place, to be known to posterity as Hothampton. He spent £60,000; he erected and furnished some really commodious villas, but did not succeed in giving his name to his own creation, and died broken-hearted in 1799. It is interesting to note, however, that one of the best streets in Bognor is known as Hotham Place. The Local Board have expended £14,000 on a sea-wall and fine esplanade, and the pier, 1,000ft in length, cost £5,000. For a Sussex watering-place Bognor is remarkably quiet, but it will doubtless commend itself to some people on this account.

Main picture:
Bognor, Rough Seas, from the Pier 1890 25182b
Below:
Bognor, The Beach Hotel 1898 42584
Far right:
Bognor, The Beach 1890 22626

Littlehampton

Littlehampton, The Beach 1898 42574

What shall we say about Littlehampton? What can be said, except that it lies between Worthing and Bognor; and that it is, perhaps, quieter than either; that children will find a paradise upon its sands, with nothing from which they can contrive to tumble; and that some older young folk may be inclined to grumble if asked to spend their holiday there? - though there can be no doubt that Littlehampton has grown far livelier within the last few years. The air is mild - rather too much so for some tastes. The neighbourhood is flat and the soil sandy. The houses stand some way back, and are separated from the sea by a strip of green sward, broken with undulations and clumps of firs, which make this spot a capital playground. There is no pleasure pier at Littlehampton, but there is a jetty and a good parade provided with sheltered seats.

Southsea, The Beach 1892 30017

Southsea

A s practically the west-end of Portsmouth, Southsea holds a unique position among watering-places. It would not be rustic or romantic enough for all tastes, but recommends itself to many by the stir of military and naval life. What with regimental bands, parades, and reviews by land, and the Solent continually alive with yachts, steamboats, and battleships, it can never be dull; nor is it surprising that not a few old officers think there is no place like Southsea for a permanent or temporary residence. Leading from the Esplanade to the shingly beach is the bathing stage of the Portsmouth Swimming Club, which is well appreciated by swimmers. One may reach the Isle of Wight by steamer in less than half an hour, and there are also excursions by water to Southampton and Bournemouth. At the head of the harbour is Portchester Castle, now a fine and extensive ruin. The top of Portsdown Hill, which is not far from

Southsea, The Parade 1890 22771

here, affords a beautiful view of the Isle of Wight, and is greatly resorted to by visitors. Netley Abbey, on the shores of Southampton Water, although some thirteen miles off, is also a very delightful place for excursionists.

Main picture:
Southsea,
The Beach and Pier
1898 42693

Top left:
Southsea,
The Beach 1890
22774

Top right: *Southsea,*
The Beach and Pier
1890 22761

Ryde, IOW

Ryde, The Pier 1899 44304

This is practically the chief town of the Isle of Wight, and the centre of the summer season. The scenery is very beautiful, and the picturesque houses and gardens rise, 'as spectators in an amphitheatre', upwards from the sea, and have at times an august spectacle to look upon, in the assemblage of British fleets off Spithead. The popularity of Ryde seems to be increasing; stuccoed houses and villas are springing up in every direction, heightening, rather than deteriorating, as too frequently the case, the general beauty of the place by their being embowered among trees and in their own gardens. Ryde dates the beginning of its prosperity from the construction of its pier, which was commenced by a joint-stock company in 1813. The cheerful and picturesque esplanade was constructed in 1856, by carrying the roadway along a marshy meadow, in which were buried the bodies of the unfortunate crew of the 'Royal George'.

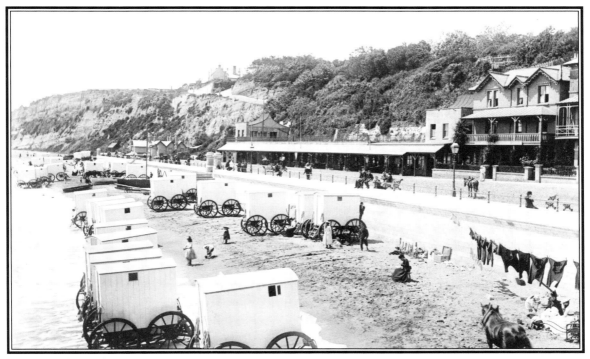

Sandown, The Beach 1892 30048

Sandown, IOW

The visitor to the Isle of Wight a few years ago would have found no Sandown at all, only a lovely horse-shoe bay paved with solid, shining sand, a few fishermen's cottages, and a half-drowned fort. Now it is one of the most popular resorts in the island, thanks to the railway, its lovely situation, and perfect bathing accommodation. A large number of hotels, lodging-houses, and shops now fringe the shore; and a small but elegant pier has recently been added. Occupying a break in the line of cliffs of iron-sand and dark coloured clays, which form the sides of the ample bay, it enjoys the benefit of the inland breeze as well as the sea air, and is consequently less oppressively hot than Shanklin. The visitor to Sandown must not be repelled by the first aspect, which is somewhat bleak, owing to the

Sandown, A Victorian Family 1895 36250X

absence of trees; and, moreover, as the cliff does not rise immediately behind the town, it can never be so pretty or so picturesque a place as Bonchurch or Ventnor. It is one of the most delightful resorts in the United Kingdom.

Ventnor, IOW

This is the capital of the Undercliff. Its popularity is due to the remarkable salubrity of its climate, and the singular beauty of its situation. 'Forty years ago', says one authority, 'Ventnor contained about half-a-dozen humble cottages; and until the publication of Sir James Clark's work (which, by the way, bore the portentous name of "The Influence of Climate in Prevention and Cure of Disease"), its few inhabitants were nearly all fishermen'. Now we have hotels, churches, shops, cottages and villas in every conceivable style and every outrageous shape. From the Esplanade there extends a fine pier, erected by the Local Board in 1887, and from which steamboat excursions may be made to Bournemouth and Brighton. The Downs above Ventnor can be reached by a road leading from near the railway station. Ventnor is essentially a place that has been made by doctors, and nothing can be more astonishing than the rapidity with which the tiny fishing hamlet was transformed into a fashionable resort.

Main picture: *Ventnor, The Beach 1899* 43138
Below: *Ventnor, The Esplanade from the New Pavilion 1896* 37214
Above left: *Ventnor, The Esplanade 1892* 30061

Bournemouth, Invalid's Walk 1900 45225

Bournemouth, East Cliff 1897 40562

Bournemouth

In position and aspect, Bournemouth is unique among English watering-places. From the evergreen valley of the Bourne (whence arose the nucleus of this resort) it stretches for miles in either direction upon the sandy cliffs and pine-clad tableland of a gently curving bay, broken by picturesque chines. Not a few of the residences in Bournemouth are fine mansions standing in extensive and beautiful grounds. From this select sojourn of delicate ease the working elements of society are for the most part banished to villages and cottages inland and out of sight, so that the town itself, instead of being shut in by shabby suburbs, is at most points fringed by pinewoods and moors. The pier projects from the seafront between East and West Cliffs, at the mouth of the Bourne Valley, and was erected in 1878 at a cost of £22,000. Nothing can be more snug and luxuriant than the mouth of the valley, which is here being turned into a long strip of garden, blooming

Bournemouth, West Cliff from the East 1897 40558

with arbutus, rhododendrons and other choice shrubs. The climate of Bournemouth is perhaps most beneficial to invalids during the fall of the year and the early spring, when it will compare favourably with many of the Mediterranean resorts.

Swanage, From the Pier 1897 40301

Swanage

Since the opening of the railway, Swanage has vastly increased in favour as a watering-place; it is situated in a beautiful bay, and commands a glorious prospect of down and sea and cliff. Swanage is shut in by a range of chalk hills, about 700ft high, and the coast is indented with numerous wide coves. The Purbeck peninsula is 12 miles long, and near here, in a deep central valley, lie the mossy ruins of Corfe Castle. The town of Swanage is unpretending, and its patrons will be those who do not crave for gaiety. Beyond its attraction as a family watering-place, the great interest of the neighbourhood is for the geologist. In the neighbourhood lie upwards of sixty quarries of Purbeck stone, which have contributed a great part of the material employed in St Paul's Cathedral and Salisbury Cathedral.

Swanage, The Beach 1899 43762

Lulworth Cove 1894 34570

Lulworth Cove

Lulworth Cove is a sheltered nook of exquisite beauty, which has no equal on the Dorsetshire coast. It possesses a depth at low water of 21ft, and its basin is nearly a mile in circumference, sheltered by lofty cliffs of sand and chalk. From a cavern below the little watering-place there flows a clear stream, which after supplying a flour-mill, ripples downward into a cove. Lulworth is a typical seaside village, and is well adapted for holiday-seekers in search of peace and quietude.

Lulworth Cove, West Point 1894 34575

Weymouth

This popular watering-place is very pleasantly situated. The coast here, turning to the south, forms a wide, open bay, shaped in the form of the letter E, the projection in the centre dividing it into two parts, namely, Weymouth Bay and Portland Roads. To the north of this projecting point lies the old town of Weymouth, and connected with it, by a swing bridge across the harbour, is Melcombe Regis, the modern town, extending nearly a mile along the curving shore. Its principal feature is the esplanade, which extends along the shore of the peninsula for about a mile, and is lined with elegant houses and defended by a substantial sea-wall. At the northern end of the esplanade are the Green Hill Gardens, and at the southern end, the Alexandra Gardens; while near the clock tower stands an equestrian statue of George III, erected by the townspeople in 1809.

Main picture:
Weymouth, The Beach Show 1899 43853X
Below:
Weymouth, The Parade 1898 41119
Top right:
Weymouth, The Harbour 1898 41114

Budleigh Salterton

Budleigh Salterton, The Promenade 1898 42448

This charmingly-situated little watering-place lies in a sheltered valley, and its garden-girt villas are further beautified by a sparkling brook, spanned by numerous rustic bridges. Myrtles and hydrangeas bloom lustily in the open air in this delightful spot. The sheltered esplanade is a unique recommendation, and the beach is famous for its prettily-marked pebbles, which are so smooth that artists sometimes use them to paint upon. An omnibus runs four times a day to Exmouth, five miles away, so as to meet the trains. Among the chief attractions of the neighbourhood are Ladram Bay and the lofty cliffs near Otter Point. It is indeed a charming little spot, which thanks to the absence of the railway, retains much of its primitive simplicity. The River Otter may be crossed by a wooden bridge half a mile from the sea, and then the tourist may go on to Budleigh, a true Devonshire village with its 'cob' cottages.

Exmouth, The Pier 1896 37624

Exmouth

❧

his is a good old fashionable watering-place, with a south front that faces the open sea; an excellent beach and warm, red cliffs, round which runs a pleasant walk to Budleigh Salterton. The country behind presents exceedingly pleasant uplands of the Devonshire type, the mingling of luxuriant woods and meadows, with broken heaths and wild banks of verdure. Exmouth is provided with baths, bathing machines, libraries, assembly-rooms, archery and lawn tennis grounds, public gardens, and golf links. The sea wall, constructed from the designs of Mr Plewse in 1841-2, is 1,840ft long, 22ft high, and affords a really admirable promenade. In the centre of the town there is a pleasure ground known as the Strand Enclosure, presented some years ago by the Hon Mark Rolle; and this, together with the Manor grounds, recently acquired by the District Council, adds to the freshness and beauty of the place. The railway service

Exmouth, The Sands 1890 26261

is excellent, there being an average of a dozen trains each way daily between Exmouth and Exeter. These trains run in connection with the through main line expresses to Waterloo, from which terminus Exmouth is 182 miles distant.

Dawlish

Dawlish, The Seafront from the Royal Hotel 1890 26059

This deservedly favourite seaside resort lies in a cove formed by the projecting headlands, Langstone Cliff on the north, and the Parson and Clerk Rocks on the south. Through the bosom of the valley which here opens out by the sea, runs a crystal rivulet, spanned by numerous bridges. On the hill slopes beyond are perched numerous fantastic villas, and the Strand and the Teignmouth Road are gay with terraces, hotels and 'marine mansions'. In the Strand and up the valley towards what is called Dawlish Waters, the climate has almost an Italian geniality, and the tender myrtle and other delicate plants bloom freely in the open air. There is excellent bathing, and beautiful drives may be taken up the valley at the back of the town, between the rows of elm trees to the summit of Great Haldon, where extensive views will repay the visitor.

Torquay, From Vane Hill 1901 47806

Torquay

A celebrated art critic has declared that Edinburgh, Venice, and Torquay are the three most beautiful towns in Europe. This celebrated and fashionable winter resort occupies the northern corner of Tor Bay, and is securely sheltered from all winds, except those from the south-east. It is bounded on one side by Berry Head, a high promontory, and on the other, at a distance of more than four miles, by the headland called Hope's Nose. Torquay is a town of charming villas, which amphitheatre-like, stretch upwards from the shore in terraces to the higher ground overlooking the sea. The sweetest little inlet between Teignmouth and Dartmouth is Anstey's Cove. It is a deep and rugged recess in the cliffs, wrought out, probably, by the action of the water and the consequent subsidence of land. The rocks, with the variegated tints of marble, limestone, and shale; the dancing waters of the cove, with the little belt of shining yellow sand;

Torquay, Anstey's Cove 1896 38609

and the ferns and wild flowers – all contribute to the beauty. From Babbacombe arrangements may be made for a trip to Oddicombe Bay which has of recent years sprung into popular favour, and indeed, its natural charms and splendid bathing facilities were bound to produce such a result.

Main picture:
*Torquay, Oddicombe
Beach 1889* 21491

Above:
*Torquay,
The Strand 1906*
54015

Left:
*Torquay,
Vane Hill 1896*
38593

Paignton

This watering-place may be described as a handsome and extensive suburb of Torquay. Of late it has been greatly improved; a promenade pier has been erected, and the Esplanade - on which there is a band-stand - greatly extended. This charming resort should be visited in the apple blossoming season, for the cider apple is largely cultivated in the neighbourhood, and cider is manufactured on a large scale. Originally some distance from the sea, Paignton has now approached it, and like its fashionable neighbour, Torquay, it is rapidly extending in every direction. The town is, however, very old, having belonged to the See of Exeter from a period before the Conquest. The remains of the Bishop's Palace adjoin the churchyard. Like Torquay, Paignton possesses splendid climate and remarkably fine sands. The bathing, too, is excellent; the surrounding country is fertile and well wooded, abounding in the combes which are so characteristic of the district.

Main picture:
Paignton, The Harbour 1890 25907
Below:
Paignton, The Bathing Beach 1896 38545

Main picture:
Paignton,
The North Sands
from the Pier 1896
38549

Top right: *Paignton,*
The Pier and Sands
1896 38560

Top left:
Paignton,
The Esplanade 1896
38558

Plymouth

T here is no sea port in England that has a higher interest than Plymouth. It is more especially the great national harbour – the principal nursery of our fleet. Starting from any of the hotels, the visitor to Plymouth should visit the Hoe, the Citadel, and the Municipal Buildings, after which he may with advantage undertake the longer excursion to Mount Edgcumbe, the breakwater, Cawsand, Saltram, and up the Tamar. The Hoe, a slight but commanding elevation partly covered with grass, which overlooks Mill Bay and the Sound, is one of the features of Plymouth. Along its summit runs the favourite promenade of the Plymouth people. The view comprises Mount Edgcumbe, St Nicholas Island, Devonport and Stonehouse. Mount Edgcumbe is undoubtedly the loveliest spot in the immediate vicinity of Plymouth. It is at the extreme end of a promontory, four or five miles long, and has been carefully cultivated into a beautiful and extensive pleasure garden.

Main picture: *Plymouth, The Pier 1898* 41930
Below: *Plymouth, The Barbican 1890* 22474

Falmouth

Falmouth, The Beach 1895 37044

During the last ten years the beauties of Falmouth have become better known. The landowners and townspeople generally, whilst not paying less attention to shipping - for which Falmouth has always been famous - are rapidly developing the many eligible building sites, and erecting thereon large and commodious houses and charming terraces, which overlook the harbour. The effect is very striking. The old town, quaint and picturesque, is situate on the low ground near the edge of the harbour, and as a matter of course, the streets are very narrow. The new portion of the town lies for the most part on high ground, overlooking the magnificent harbour on the one side and the English Channel on the other. The history of Falmouth really commences with the building of Pendennis Castle, which was erected about the year 1538 by command of Henry VIII. The beautiful Castle Drive forms an esplanade the like of which is not to be met with in the kingdom. The most charming trip to be made from Falmouth is unquestionably that up the River Fal to Truro.

Penzance, The Esplanade 1890 27690a

Penzance

Penzance is celebrated as a watering-place on account of its mild climate, which makes it the resort of invalids suffering from pulmonary complaints. The old town, spread picturesquely round part of Mount's Bay, has delightfully narrow streets that ascend the hill from the fine esplanade at the edge of the sea. Mount's Bay is an expanse of sea contained within the headlands of Tol-Pedn-Penwith, west of Penzance, and the Lizard, which looms in the blue distance, twenty miles off, to the east. Since the seventies a new quarter has sprung up to westward, with really fine modern streets, for the accommodation of visitors. Such thoroughfares are the Trewithen, Morrab and Alexandra Roads. The esplanade is a broad, asphalted walk along the shore, with baths at the West-end; and at the other end what are known as the Battery Rocks, of greenstone. The esplanade commands a beautiful view over the fine expanse of

St Michael's Mount 1891 36179

Mount's Bay, margined by a semi-circle of low hills, in front of which stands out the splendid pyramid of St Michael's Mount, a striking feature of a noble prospect, that is also frequently enlivened by the departure of the fleet of the fishing-boats for which the district is famed.

Newquay, From the Fish Cellars 1887 20244

Newquay, Towan Beach 1901 47734

Newquay

The Great Western Railway found Newquay a small and almost inaccessible Cornish fishing village, and have transformed it into quite a fashionable seaside resort, containing nearly 3,000 inhabitants. It is now the terminus of the branch line from Par Junction. Newquay lies at the western end of Watergate Bay, under the shelter of Towan Head – a grand promontory and fine point of view, reached by the path across Beacon Hill. The splendid sandy beach, which is so firm that tennis may be played on it, extends eastward for three miles beneath a range of beautiful cliffs. Although this grand coast is usually visited in the summer, the best time to study its stern, impressive beauty is during the winter season, when the long, crested waves dash themselves against the keen-edged rocks, and the misty rain and salt spray drive inland before the wind, the only spectator being the raven, whose croaking is intermittently heard in the roar of the breakers. The

Newquay, The Beach 1901 47733

pilchard fishery here employs a great number of hands from July to November, when the shoals disappear as suddenly as they come. Fistral Beach is studded with rocks, pools and ledges that are the delight of juvenile naturalists.

Main picture:
*Newquay,
The Harbour 1894*
33521

Above:
*Newquay,
The Sands 1887*
20237

Top left:
*Newquay,
On the Sands and
the Great Western
Hotel 1887* 20249

Bude, Chapel Rock 1890 23792

Bude

Bude is a very quiet, modern little place, founded by the late Sir Thomas Acland, and consisting of a few rows of small, white lodging-houses, two hotels, and some detached villas, with the attraction of excellent golf links, which draw visitors in the autumn. It stands about half a mile from the sea, at a place where a rupture in the cliffs, here lining the coast, has formed a sandy creek or bay. The vast and picturesque sea cliffs in this part of Cornwall, by the way, are a great attraction to Bude, and the climate is far dryer and more free from fog than most parts of the county. The bathing here is not very good. The tides are too violent for machines, and therefore canvas tents are erected on the sands for the use of the bathers, who have to encounter high and heavy billows rolling in from the Atlantic. The shore is, however, shallow for some distance out. The points most calculated to delight and astonish the traveller are the headlands of

Bude, Barrel Rock 1893 31915

Hennacliff, to the north of Bude, and the Dazard, the western boundary of Widemouth Bay.

Ilfracombe

Ilfracombe, Wildersmouth Beach 1899 43114

Ilfracombe is almost encircled by picturesque, verdurous heights of tors, and is remarkable for a peculiar form of coast, rarely to be met with elsewhere. Land and sea together combine in making constant alternations of high, craggy, furze-crowned tors, in some cases almost overhanging the sea below. Some serve as landmarks to seamen. Ilfracombe is hardly the best place for children, the promenade here being on rocky cliffs and not on safe sands. The bathing arrangements here are peculiar. At Crewkhorne one passes under the Runnycleaves by a dark tunnel that casts a shade of serious resolve upon the would-be bather, and on the hottest day inspires a shiver premonitory of the coming plunge. This Avernus-like entrance opens out into a picturesque cove, containing two walled-in bathing pools for ladies and gentlemen. Perhaps no better testimony to the salubrity of Ilfracombe can be adduced from the fact that the parish church contains memorial stones to eight reputed centenarians.

Main picture:
Ilfracombe,
The Harbour c1890
I50001

Above: *Ilfracombe,*
Capstone Parade
1894 33440

Weston-super-Mare

Situated some twenty miles west of Bristol on the Great Western Railway, Weston may be reached within three and a half hours from Paddington. It began to develop into a watering-place in the year 1811. At the last census it showed a resident population of 15,529, which number is, of course, more than doubled during the summer season, the Midlands contributing a large proportion of the visitors. In addition to pure air, Weston has an unlimited supply of pure water from a never-failing spring, owned by the town, which is said to have its source in the Mendip range of hills. There are lovely roads and drives in the immediate neighbourhood, notably through the woods, and around Worlebury Hill. The town possesses one of the most extensive, and certainly one of the safest, bathing beaches in the kingdom; in short, we cannot hope to enumerate even a tithe of the attractions of this charming resort in the very small space at our disposal.

Main picture: *Weston-super-Mare, The Sands 1887* 20318
Below: *Weston-super-Mare, On the Beach 1896* 38453
Top left: *Weston-super-Mare, Glentworth Bay 1887* 20324

Clevedon, The Green Beach 1892 31252

Clevedon

This delightful and fashionable watering-place is about fifteen miles from Bristol. As a health resort it occupies a very prominent place, whilst its immunity from the heavy excursion element which affects many seaside towns renders it a veritable haven of rest, commending itself each year more and more to professional men and others from Bristol. Clevedon is snugly situated with the broad expanse of the Bristol Channel open to its western front. The most popular and fashionable part of the promenade is that known as the Green Beach. It consists of an extensive plateau of greensward, about 40ft above the shelving beach, and provided with an elegant band-stand, a plantation, and a very handsome drinking-fountain. The esplanade is a continuation of the sea-front, and extends northward to the pier, which was originally opened in 1869 having cost £12,000. It was re-opened by Lady Elton in 1893, after improvements.

Clevedon, The Pier 1892 31251

Penarth

Penarth, The Beach 1896 38462

What the Mumbles are to Swansea, Penarth is to Cardiff, of which it may almost be considered a suburb. Twenty years ago it might have passed as the type of a dismal, forlorn resort, with the one solitary advantage of a good look-out onto the busy Bristol Channel. Of late, considerable improvements have been made, and it now stands in high favour. Frequent steamboats ply across the harbour when the tide serves. Penarth stands on a breezy cliff, where fine pleasure grounds have been laid out. The bathing is not to be praised, the water being muddy and the beach very shingly. The Windsor Gardens, above the esplanade, afford pleasant walks and views, but a more extensive panorama is commanded from Penarth Head itself. Penarth was, until quite recently, merely the marine residence and bathing resort of the well-to-do inhabitants of Cardiff; now, however, it bids fair to become of far more than local importance.

Main picture:
Penarth,
The Sands 1893
32689

Above:
Penarth,
View of the Seafront
from the Pier 1896
38464

Tenby

Tenby stands on a tongue of limestone rock, ending in a green promontory, which is crowned by the ruins of the old castle, and is now pleasantly laid out with walks which serve at once as pier and promenade, and from which are commanded fine views of the bays on either hand, of the bluff islands in front, and of the distant Devonshire coast opposite. The sea front of the town stands imposingly displayed on the brow of the cliffs; and masses of ruined walls and arches have a fine effect, half revealed as they are among the modern streets. The beautiful transparent greens and blues of the sea, viewed from these cliffs, are another remarkable feature. Both on the north and south sands, which are separated from each other by the Castle Hill and harbour, there are numerous bathing machines; and it should be mentioned that in this respect Tenby is above reproach. The trade of the port is not extensive, and most of the vessels frequenting the harbour belong to other places. Caldy Island, two and a half miles from Tenby Harbour, is frequently visited in boats and its beach and cliffs receive numerous picnic parties.

Main picture: *Tenby, The Harbour 1890* 28041
Below: *Tenby, On the Beach 1890* 28062

Lydstep

Lydstep, The Beach 1890 28010X

This is pre-eminently one of those places which have to be 'discovered', so to speak, by the roving holiday-maker. A prospective tourist not unfrequently takes considerable trouble to find out some charming seaside village in which he may dream out his few brief weeks of leisure in ineffable content and rest, soothed by the ever-present, placid sea, the rugged, flower-clad cliffs, and the charming, old-world life that goes on around him. To such is unhesitatingly recommended the delightful place shown in this view. The quiet and beautiful village of Lydstep is about three miles from Tenby, and offers bathing facilities that cannot be surpassed. Near the village are some remarkable caves on the coast, which may, however, only be visited at certain states of the tide. The whole of the coast scenery hereabouts is very grand, commencing with Proud Giltar, with its sheer face of rock rising perpendicular from the ocean.

Aberystwyth

Aberystwyth, Victoria Promenade 1899 44527

Not so picturesque in its background as Barmouth, not so select as Tenby, and not so lively as Llandudno, Aberystwyth has hardly the right to proclaim herself 'the Queen of Welsh Watering Places', as she rather arrogantly does. Since the completion of the railway, great improvements have been made here, one of the most important of these being the construction of Victoria Terrace, by which means the Marine Terrace has been completed from Castlepoint to Craiglais. From a sanitary point of view, Aberystwyth has made vast strides. The Corporation have introduced into the town an unlimited supply of pure water from a natural lake below Plynlimmon. The pride of Aberystwyth is its ruined castle, crumbling upon a rocky promontory against whose sides the waves of every tide are dashed with a force that threatens eventually to sweep away the whole.

Abersytwyth,
The Promenade and
Beach 1899 44525

Rhyl

Not many years ago there was no town here at all, but merely a few fishermen's huts upon the shore. The sands, which are extensive enough to give the full benefit of ozone to those who avail themselves of its health-giving properties, form an excellent bathing-ground, entirely free from danger. Hence Rhyl has become noted for the number of children that visit it, and these little ones find an inexhaustible fund of pleasure on its beach. The iron pier at this watering-place was built in 1867, and cost about £23,000. It is 785yds in length, and towards the end of 1891 a grand pavilion was erected at the entrance, capable of seating 2,5000 persons. Behind the stage in this building is erected one of the largest organs in England, that of the Manchester Exhibition, by Messrs Bishop and Son. Rhyl has exceedingly beautiful inland attractions. Its situation is at the mouth of the River Clwyd, and the Valley of the Clwyd is one of the most charming of all the Welsh valleys.

Main picture:
Rhyl, The Sands 1891 29151
Below:
Rhyl, The Pavilion and Pier c1865 2254

Pwllheli, West End Promenade 1898 42409

Pwllheli

This watering-place is beautifully situated on the shores of Cardigan Bay. It is the terminus of the coast section of the Cambrian Railways. Pwllheli possesses perhaps the finest sandy beach in Wales; and there can be no doubt it will become one of the most attractive seaside places in the kingdom. The air is delightful, and the sanitary arrangements all that could be desired. It has a southern aspect, and is sheltered from cold winds by the encircling mountains on the north and east sides. The wide esplanade facing the sea was constructed a few years ago. The South Beach Land and Building Corporation Limited, are building very extensively; and hotels, boarding and private houses are now being erected very rapidly. River fishing abounds at Pwllheli, and a boating excursion, in fine weather, to Bardsea, is a very enjoyable trip.

Pwllheli, General View 1891 29559

Llanfairfechan

Llanfairfechan, The Sands 1890 23214

This lovely little spot lies rather to the west of Penmaenmawr, whose advantages it certainly shares. Although Llanfairfechan is eclipsed by its more pretentious neighbour, it is regarded with increasing favour by tourists and holiday-makers, who frequent the out-of-the-way parts of Wales. As may be seen in this view, this charming little watering-place may be described as having a wooded and well-sheltered situation at the foot of the Penmaenmawr Mountain, and with a singularly lovely seaward prospect. No great crowds of holiday-makers are seen in our illustration, but the astute observer may discern significant signs of the rising watering-place.

Llanfairfechan, The Sands 1890 23212

Llandudno

There is something unique in the situation of Llandudno. It stands back against the mass of the Great Orme's Head, which shelters it from north winds, and on a neck of sand between two bays, which are so close together that in rough weather their spray meets over the town. The outer bay has a fine sweep, fringed with a long promenade and crescent extending towards the lower and more broken heights of the Little Orme. The Great Orme has now been encircled by a good carriage road. On reaching the old telegraph station at an altitude of 750ft, the persevering tourist is rewarded by a magnificent bird's-eye view of Llandudno beneath. The bright blue waters of the sea, the hills of Gloddaeth, the majestic ruins and bridges of Conway, all combine to form a prospect of wondrous beauty, which, bounded by the undulating outlines of the mountains, is well worth a pilgrimage to contemplate.

Main picture:
Llandudno, The Pier 1890 23250
Below:
Llandudno, The Beach 1891 29430

*Llandudno,
On the Beach 1890*
23242

Colwyn Bay, The Pier Pavilion 1900 46268

Colwyn Bay, On the Sands 1898 42375

Colwyn Bay

Colwyn Bay, The New Promenade 1897 40031

From Rhyl to Carnarvon and away down the coast are springing up towns and villages, all in the main catering for the vast army of health and pleasure seekers who annually wend their way to the seaside for days, weeks, or months. Of the fine climate of Colwyn Bay there can be no doubt whatever. Flowers bloom here until well on towards Christmas, and are out again in some profusion in February. The gently-sloping sands extend for a mile or two, and perfectly safe for children; while the deep water wherein the expert swimmer loves to disport himself is not too far out to be tiresome. The views of sea and coast are very fine, and this watering-place possesses the comparatively rare advantage of being beautifully wooded, the very streets resembling fine boulevards, and the surrounding district affording lovely walks along the rising and well-wooded slopes. The thriving town of Colwyn Bay must not be confounded with the village of Colwyn, or Old Colwyn, as it is commonly called to distinguish it from the modern resort. The town is situated on the Chester and Holyhead line of railway, and is very conveniently placed for short excursions to many other of the best-known pleasure resorts in North Wales.

New Brighton, The Tower 1898 40902

New Brighton, The Beach 1887 20067

New Brighton

If the truth must be told, we fancy that few readers would care to be recommended to New Brighton, except Liverpool people, who already know enough about a place lying so close at hand; but we may mention that this is the chief Mersey bathing-place, which at once gains and loses by its proximity to the great commercial city. There are here a commodious pier, and a sandy beach well supplied with bathing machines, donkeys, nigger minstrels, and the like attractions for the amusement of the Bank Holiday crowds. New Brighton is built on rising ground, five miles to the north-west of Birkenhead. The pier is 560ft long, and affords fine views of the shipping and docks of Liverpool, the Irish Sea, and the mountains of Wales. The railway line from Liverpool passes under the river by the Mersey Tunnel; it was begun in 1880, and opened for traffic in 1886.

New Brighton, The Pier 1900 45165

Blackpool

As Justice Shallow might say, Blackpool has two piers, and everything handsome about her. Both are large; the north one is the more select, and the south more popular – just a penny pier where dancing goes on all day in the summer. The promenade is lighted by electricity, and has an electric tramway. Not to be left behind in any respect, Blackpool now has an Eiffel Tower of its own. A rate was raised for the purpose of giving the town's attractions wide advertisement through the medium of handbills and flaring posters; one would hardly think, however, that this was the best way of drawing the most satisfactory class of visitors to 'the finest promenade in England'. Standing solidly upon a low range of cliffs, facing the Irish Sea, Blackpool enjoys its briny breezes for nine months of the year. At low tide the grasping waves retire nearly half a mile, leaving a stretch of sand nearly twenty miles in length. The amusements on this extensive beach include riding and driving.

Main picture:
Blackpool, The South Pier 1890 22881
Below:
Blackpool, From the Pier 1896 38839

Main picture:
Blackpool, Central Beach 1890 22870

Top left: *Blackpool, The Sands 1890* 22883

Top right: *Blackpool, The Central Beach 1890* 22869

Morecambe

Morecambe, The Promenade 1899 42860

Morecambe is much frequented by trippers from the busy towns of Lancashire and Yorkshire, for whose recreation are provided abundant entertainments of a distinctly popular order. There are swimming-baths and assembly-rooms - of a sort - a People's Palace, and a few other places of amusement, chiefly conducted on music-hall lines. There is a large pier, a tramway, and a kind of Rosherville Garden with a lake for boating. There are strawberry gardens in the neighbourhood; and Morecambe is provided with whole fleets of pleasure boats and excursion steamers. Covered bazaars and open-air stalls form a characteristic feature of the streets. Promenade Pier was opened in 1869. It is built entirely of iron, and extends 612ft into the bay. It is said that this pier has cost altogether about £15,000, but this does not appear a very large sum when we consider that 4,000 persons can comfortably disport themselves on it at one time.

Grange-over-Sands, Playing Tennis 1894 34116

Grange-over-Sands

Grange-over-Sands, The Beach 1896 38516

A scattering of mansions, cottages, and odds and ends of streets nestling beneath a limestone cliff or half hidden away among wooded slopes, this tiny Torquay of Lancashire has, as yet, escaped the notice it fairly deserves. Looking southward over the wide sands of Morecambe Bay from the promontory between the Kent and Leven estuaries, sheltered by hills, upon a soil of limestone and gravel, it has a climate worthy of its natural charms. Except at high tide, we find here an expanse of mud and wet channelled sand, where bathers and boaters are fain, indeed, to snatch a fleeting joy. Only at certain hours is the jetty accessible to the steamboats that come across from Morecambe. On such occasions, however, one may take a short trip, and thereby obtain a beautiful view of the wooded shore. The principal inland attraction is the walk to Hampsfell Hill, an easy hour's climb of about 800ft. At the top will be found a square tower commanding a view that takes in Ingleborough, Carnforth, Lancaster, Morecambe Bay and the smoke of Barrow. From Grange one may reach Lakeside, Bowness, or Kendal in a few hours.

Arnside

Arnside has not, perhaps, such fine views of the Bay as may be obtained from Grange. This place can be thoroughly 'done' in a very short time. The visitor to Arnside will, however, notice the substantial appearance of the neat villas, houses, and shops; the firm and excellent sands, on which the children are at play; and the delightful situation of the town on the slope and at the foot of the hill known as Arnside Knot. A little stone pier projects from the promenade, and from it the pleasure-boats put off. A notable feature of the estuary is the rapidity with which the flood tide covers the vast expanse of sands here, so that one runs some little risk in rambling over the sands too far away from the shore. This charming little place is developing very rapidly, and is already a formidable rival to its popular neighbour, Grange-over-Sands.

Main picture:
Arnside, From the Beach 1894 34128
Below:
Arnside, The Beach 1894 34130
Top left:
Arnside, The Beach 1891 28645

Ramsey, IOM

This charming watering-place is a well-built and eminently respectable town, quiet and healthy, surrounded by most attractive scenery, and in every way a suitable place for those who are in search of invigorating air and other seaside advantages in full measure. Fish and vegetables are abundant, cheap and varied. Horses may be hired, and there are troops of the meekest of meek donkeys for the children. As regards the bathing, we may mention that the water is beautifully transparent, and the sands broad and free from quicksands, holes, or other dangers to bathers. The bathing machines and boats are kept on the south shore of this resort. From the south pier at Ramsey a broad, asphalted promenade extends southward about 2,000ft to the principal pier, which is 2,200ft in length. Steamers arriving at Ramsey usually land their passengers at the Queen's Pier, while occasionally at high tides the vessels go right into the harbour.

Main picture: *Ramsey, The Town 1895* 36739
Below: *Ramsey, The Seafront 1894* 33059
Top left: *Ramsey, The Beach 1893* 33061

Douglas, IOM

Douglas is well supplied with all ordinary requisites, excellent hotels, piers, and promenades. At Douglas, passengers can land at all states of the tide. The bay has been compared by local enthusiasts to the Bay of Naples, because at night a long crescent of lights is seen rising from the water. On the south side are the handsome stone piers, and a deep harbour cutting off most of the town from the cliffs of Douglas Head. Here lies the old town, whose narrow and crooked streets have been cloaked, so to speak, by the fine sea front spreading round to the north end. A fine broad street of handsome shops connects the shore with the upper part of the town. The northern stone pier is known as the Old Pier; the lighthouse here shows a white light at night, and a red ball by day, whenever there is a depth of 9ft in the harbour. The latter shelters fully 200 Manx boats.

Main picture:
Douglas, The Promenade 1897 39882
Below:
Douglas, The Promenade 1895 36727
Top right:
Douglas, The New Tramway Station 1896 38771a

Rothesay

H ere we have the chief town of the County of Bute; it contains 9,034 inhabitants, and is situated in a well-formed bay, which affords safe anchorage in high wind. A fine esplanade faces the bay, and is laid out with much taste; it commands many beautiful views of Loch Striven. In the centre of the town are the ruins of Rothesay Castle, once a royal residence, and said to have been built about the year 1100. On the east side of the island, five miles from Rothesay, is Mount Stewart, the seat of the Marquess of Bute. On leaving Rothesay by steamer, one passes on the left Bannatyne and the bay, and Castle Kames, after which one enters the Kyles of Bute, a sound or strait lying between the north part of Bute and the district of Cowal.

Main picture:
Rothesay, The Pier 1897 39836
Below:
Rothesay, Port Bannatyne 1897 39842

Largs

Largs, The Beach 1897 39856

This well-known Scottish resort may be reached by the Glasgow and South-Western Railway from Glasgow in about an hour and a half. Largs is a fine clean town, with several large churches, including a Gothic episcopal chapel built in 1877, which contains many painted windows. There are in Largs a great number of excellent houses for summer visitors, besides handsome and comfortable residential villas in the neighbourhood. The railway was opened in 1885. There is now a golf course here; and the shelter afforded by the Great Cumbrae makes Largs a first-rate place for boating. Behind the town lies some very high country, into which run innumerable lovely glens. Largs commands a magnificent view of Arran; and there is a railway from the town along the coast to Ardrossan, a distance of twelve miles.

Index

Frith Book Co Titles

www.francisfrith.co.uk

The Frith Book Company publishes over 100 new titles each year. A selection of those currently available is listed below. For latest catalogue please contact Frith Book Co.

Town Books 96 pages, approximately 100 photos. **County and Themed Books** 128 pages, approximately 150 photos (unless specified). All titles hardback with laminated case and jacket, except those indicated pb (paperback)

Title	ISBN	Price	Title	ISBN	Price
Amersham, Chesham & Rickmansworth (pb)	1-85937-340-2	£9.99	Devon (pb)	1-85937-297-x	£9.99
Andover (pb)	1-85937-292-9	£9.99	Devon Churches (pb)	1-85937-250-3	£9.99
Aylesbury (pb)	1-85937-227-9	£9.99	Dorchester (pb)	1-85937-307-0	£9.99
Barnstaple (pb)	1-85937-300-3	£9.99	Dorset (pb)	1-85937-269-4	£9.99
Basildon Living Memories (pb)	1-85937-515-4	£9.99	Dorset Coast (pb)	1-85937-299-6	£9.99
Bath (pb)	1-85937-419-0	£9.99	Dorset Living Memories (pb)	1-85937-584-7	£9.99
Bedford (pb)	1-85937-205-8	£9.99	Down the Severn (pb)	1-85937-560-x	£9.99
Bedfordshire Living Memories	1-85937-513-8	£14.99	Down The Thames (pb)	1-85937-278-3	£9.99
Belfast (pb)	1-85937-303-8	£9.99	Down the Trent	1-85937-311-9	£14.99
Berkshire (pb)	1-85937-191-4	£9.99	East Anglia (pb)	1-85937-265-1	£9.99
Berkshire Churches	1-85937-170-1	£17.99	East Grinstead (pb)	1-85937-138-8	£9.99
Berkshire Living Memories	1-85937-332-1	£14.99	East London	1-85937-080-2	£14.99
Black Country	1-85937-497-2	£12.99	East Sussex (pb)	1-85937-606-1	£9.99
Blackpool (pb)	1-85937-393-3	£9.99	Eastbourne (pb)	1-85937-399-2	£9.99
Bognor Regis (pb)	1-85937-431-x	£9.99	Edinburgh (pb)	1-85937-193-0	£8.99
Bournemouth (pb)	1-85937-545-6	£9.99	England In The 1880s	1-85937-331-3	£17.99
Bradford (pb)	1-85937-204-x	£9.99	Essex - Second Selection	1-85937-456-5	£14.99
Bridgend (pb)	1-85937-386-0	£7.99	Essex (pb)	1-85937-270-8	£9.99
Bridgwater (pb)	1-85937-305-4	£9.99	Essex Coast	1-85937-342-9	£14.99
Bridport (pb)	1-85937-327-5	£9.99	Essex Living Memories	1-85937-490-5	£14.99
Brighton (pb)	1-85937-192-2	£8.99	Exeter	1-85937-539-1	£9.99
Bristol (pb)	1-85937-264-3	£9.99	Exmoor (pb)	1-85937-608-8	£9.99
British Life A Century Ago (pb)	1-85937-213-9	£9.99	Falmouth (pb)	1-85937-594-4	£9.99
Buckinghamshire (pb)	1-85937-200-7	£9.99	Folkestone (pb)	1-85937-124-8	£9.99
Camberley (pb)	1-85937-222-8	£9.99	Frome (pb)	1-85937-317-8	£9.99
Cambridge (pb)	1-85937-422-0	£9.99	Glamorgan	1-85937-488-3	£14.99
Cambridgeshire (pb)	1-85937-420-4	£9.99	Glasgow (pb)	1-85937-190-6	£9.99
Cambridgeshire Villages	1-85937-523-5	£14.99	Glastonbury (pb)	1-85937-338-0	£7.99
Canals And Waterways (pb)	1-85937-291-0	£9.99	Gloucester (pb)	1-85937-232-5	£9.99
Canterbury Cathedral (pb)	1-85937-179-5	£9.99	Gloucestershire (pb)	1-85937-561-8	£9.99
Cardiff (pb)	1-85937-093-4	£9.99	Great Yarmouth (pb)	1-85937-426-3	£9.99
Carmarthenshire (pb)	1-85937-604-5	£9.99	Greater Manchester (pb)	1-85937-266-x	£9.99
Chelmsford (pb)	1-85937-310-0	£9.99	Guildford (pb)	1-85937-410-7	£9.99
Cheltenham (pb)	1-85937-095-0	£9.99	Hampshire (pb)	1-85937-279-1	£9.99
Cheshire (pb)	1-85937-271-6	£9.99	Harrogate (pb)	1-85937-423-9	£9.99
Chester (pb)	1-85937-382 8	£9.99	Hastings and Bexhill (pb)	1-85937-131-0	£9.99
Chesterfield (pb)	1-85937-378-x	£9.99	Heart of Lancashire (pb)	1-85937-197-3	£9.99
Chichester (pb)	1-85937-228-7	£9.99	Helston (pb)	1-85937-214-7	£9.99
Churches of East Cornwall (pb)	1-85937-249-x	£9.99	Hereford (pb)	1-85937-175-2	£9.99
Churches of Hampshire (pb)	1-85937-207-4	£9.99	Herefordshire (pb)	1-85937-567-7	£9.99
Cinque Ports & Two Ancient Towns	1-85937-492-1	£14.99	Herefordshire Living Memories	1-85937-514-6	£14.99
Colchester (pb)	1-85937-188-4	£8.99	Hertfordshire (pb)	1-85937-247-3	£9.99
Cornwall (pb)	1-85937-229-5	£9.99	Horsham (pb)	1-85937-432-8	£9.99
Cornwall Living Memories	1-85937-248-1	£14.99	Humberside (pb)	1-85937-605-3	£9.99
Cotswolds (pb)	1-85937-230-9	£9.99	Hythe, Romney Marsh, Ashford (pb)	1-85937-256-2	£9.99
Cotswolds Living Memories	1-85937-255-4	£14.99	Ipswich (pb)	1-85937-424-7	£9.99
County Durham (pb)	1-85937-398-4	£9.99	Isle of Man (pb)	1-85937-268-6	£9.99
Croydon Living Memories (pb)	1-85937-162-0	£9.99	Isle of Wight (pb)	1-85937-429-8	£9.99
Cumbria (pb)	1-85937-621-5	£9.99	Isle of Wight Living Memories	1-85937-304-6	£14.99
Derby (pb)	1-85937-367-4	£9.99	Kent (pb)	1-85937-189-2	£9.99
Derbyshire (pb)	1-85937-196-5	£9.99	Kent Living Memories(pb)	1-85937-401-8	£9.99
Derbyshire Living Memories	1-85937-330-5	£14.99	Kings Lynn (pb)	1-85937-334-8	£9.99

Available from your local bookshop or from the publisher

Frith Book Co Titles (continued)

Title	ISBN	Price
Lake District (pb)	1-85937-275-9	£9.99
Lancashire Living Memories	1-85937-335-6	£14.99
Lancaster, Morecambe, Heysham (pb)	1-85937-233-3	£9.99
Leeds (pb)	1-85937-202-3	£9.99
Leicester (pb)	1-85937-381-x	£9.99
Leicestershire & Rutland Living Memories	1-85937-500-6	£12.99
Leicestershire (pb)	1-85937-185-x	£9.99
Lighthouses	1-85937-257-0	£9.99
Lincoln (pb)	1-85937-380-1	£9.99
Lincolnshire (pb)	1-85937-433-6	£9.99
Liverpool and Merseyside (pb)	1-85937-234-1	£9.99
London (pb)	1-85937-183-3	£9.99
London Living Memories	1-85937-454-9	£14.99
Ludlow (pb)	1-85937-176-0	£9.99
Luton (pb)	1-85937-235-x	£9.99
Maidenhead (pb)	1-85937-339-9	£9.99
Maidstone (pb)	1-85937-391-7	£9.99
Manchester (pb)	1-85937-198-1	£9.99
Marlborough (pb)	1-85937-336-4	£9.99
Middlesex	1-85937-158-2	£14.99
Monmouthshire	1-85937-532-4	£14.99
New Forest (pb)	1-85937-390-9	£9.99
Newark (pb)	1-85937-366-6	£9.99
Newport, Wales (pb)	1-85937-258-9	£9.99
Newquay (pb)	1-85937-421-2	£9.99
Norfolk (pb)	1-85937-195-7	£9.99
Norfolk Broads	1-85937-486-7	£14.99
Norfolk Living Memories (pb)	1-85937-402-6	£9.99
North Buckinghamshire	1-85937-626-6	£14.99
North Devon Living Memories	1-85937-261-9	£14.99
North Hertfordshire	1-85937-547-2	£14.99
North London (pb)	1-85937-403-4	£9.99
North Somerset	1-85937-302-x	£14.99
North Wales (pb)	1-85937-298-8	£9.99
North Yorkshire (pb)	1-85937-236-8	£9.99
Northamptonshire Living Memories	1-85937-529-4	£14.99
Northamptonshire	1-85937-150-7	£14.99
Northumberland Tyne & Wear (pb)	1-85937-281-3	£9.99
Northumberland	1-85937-522-7	£14.99
Norwich (pb)	1-85937-194-9	£8.99
Nottingham (pb)	1-85937-324-0	£9.99
Nottinghamshire (pb)	1-85937-187-6	£9.99
Oxford (pb)	1-85937-411-5	£9.99
Oxfordshire (pb)	1-85937-430-1	£9.99
Oxfordshire Living Memories	1-85937-525-1	£14.99
Paignton (pb)	1-85937-374-7	£7.99
Peak District (pb)	1-85937-280-5	£9.99
Pembrokeshire	1-85937-262-7	£14.99
Penzance (pb)	1-85937-595-2	£9.99
Peterborough (pb)	1-85937-219-8	£9.99
Picturesque Harbours	1-85937-208-2	£14.99
Piers	1-85937-237-6	£17.99
Plymouth (pb)	1-85937-389-5	£9.99
Poole & Sandbanks (pb)	1-85937-251-1	£9.99
Preston (pb)	1-85937-212-0	£9.99
Reading (pb)	1-85937-238-4	£9.99
Redhill to Reigate (pb)	1-85937-596-0	£9.99
Ringwood (pb)	1-85937-384-4	£7.99
Romford (pb)	1-85937-319-4	£9.99
Royal Tunbridge Wells (pb)	1-85937-504-9	£9.99
Salisbury (pb)	1-85937-239-2	£9.99
Scarborough (pb)	1-85937-379-8	£9.99
Sevenoaks and Tonbridge (pb)	1-85937-392-5	£9.99
Sheffield & South Yorks (pb)	1-85937-267-8	£9.99
Sherborne (pb)	1-85937-301-1	£9.99
Shrewsbury (pb)	1-85937-325-9	£9.99
Shropshire (pb)	1-85937-326-7	£9.99
Shropshire Living Memories	1-85937-643-6	£14.99
Somerset	1-85937-153-1	£14.99
South Devon Coast	1-85937-107-8	£14.99
South Devon Living Memories (pb)	1-85937-609-6	£9.99
South East London (pb)	1-85937-263-5	£9.99
South Somerset	1-85937-318-6	£14.99
South Wales	1-85937-519-7	£14.99
Southampton (pb)	1-85937-427-1	£9.99
Southend (pb)	1-85937-313-5	£9.99
Southport (pb)	1-85937-425-5	£9.99
St Albans (pb)	1-85937-341-0	£9.99
St Ives (pb)	1-85937-415-8	£9.99
Stafford Living Memories (pb)	1-85937-503-0	£9.99
Staffordshire (pb)	1-85937-308-9	£9.99
Stourbridge (pb)	1-85937-530-8	£9.99
Stratford upon Avon (pb)	1-85937-388-7	£9.99
Suffolk (pb)	1-85937-221-x	£9.99
Suffolk Coast (pb)	1-85937-610-x	£9.99
Surrey (pb)	1-85937-240-6	£9.99
Surrey Living Memories	1-85937-328-3	£14.99
Sussex (pb)	1-85937-184-1	£9.99
Sutton (pb)	1-85937-337-2	£9.99
Swansea (pb)	1-85937-167-1	£9.99
Taunton (pb)	1-85937-314-3	£9.99
Tees Valley & Cleveland (pb)	1-85937-623-1	£9.99
Teignmouth (pb)	1-85937-370-4	£7.99
Thanet (pb)	1-85937-116-7	£9.99
Tiverton (pb)	1-85937-178-7	£9.99
Torbay (pb)	1-85937-597-9	£9.99
Truro (pb)	1-85937-598-7	£9.99
Victorian & Edwardian Dorset	1-85937-254-6	£14.99
Victorian & Edwardian Kent (pb)	1-85937-624-X	£9.99
Victorian & Edwardian Maritime Album (pb)	1-85937-622-3	£9.99
Victorian and Edwardian Sussex (pb)	1-85937-625-8	£9.99
Villages of Devon (pb)	1-85937-293-7	£9.99
Villages of Kent (pb)	1-85937-294-5	£9.99
Villages of Sussex (pb)	1-85937-295-3	£9.99
Warrington (pb)	1-85937-507-3	£9.99
Warwick (pb)	1-85937-518-9	£9.99
Warwickshire (pb)	1-85937-203-1	£9.99
Welsh Castles (pb)	1-85937-322-4	£9.99
West Midlands (pb)	1-85937-289-9	£9.99
West Sussex (pb)	1-85937-607-x	£9.99
West Yorkshire (pb)	1-85937-201-5	£9.99
Weston Super Mare (pb)	1-85937-306-2	£9.99
Weymouth (pb)	1-85937-209-0	£9.99
Wiltshire (pb)	1-85937-277-5	£9.99
Wiltshire Churches (pb)	1-85937-171-x	£9.99
Wiltshire Living Memories (pb)	1-85937-396-8	£9.99
Winchester (pb)	1-85937-428-x	£9.99
Windsor (pb)	1-85937-333-x	£9.99
Wokingham & Bracknell (pb)	1-85937-329-1	£9.99
Woodbridge (pb)	1-85937-498-0	£9.99
Worcester (pb)	1-85937-165-5	£9.99
Worcestershire Living Memories	1-85937-489-1	£14.99
Worcestershire	1-85937-152-3	£14.99
York (pb)	1-85937-199-x	£9.99
Yorkshire (pb)	1-85937-186-8	£9.99
Yorkshire Coastal Memories	1-85937-506-5	£14.99
Yorkshire Dales	1-85937-502-2	£14.99
Yorkshire Living Memories (pb)	1-85937-397-6	£9.99

See Frith books on the internet at www.francisfrith.co.uk

FRITH PRODUCTS & SERVICES

Francis Frith would doubtless be pleased to know that the pioneering publishing venture he started in 1860 still continues today. Over a hundred and forty years later, The Francis Frith Collection continues in the same innovative tradition and is now one of the foremost publishers of vintage photographs in the world. Some of the current activities include:

Interior Decoration

Today Frith's photographs can be seen framed and as giant wall murals in thousands of pubs, restaurants, hotels, banks, retail stores and other public buildings throughout the country. In every case they enhance the unique local atmosphere of the places they depict and provide reminders of gentler days in an increasingly busy and frenetic world.

Product Promotions

Frith products are used by many major companies to promote the sales of their own products or to reinforce their own history and heritage. Frith promotions have been used by Hovis bread, Courage beers, Scots Porage Oats, Colman's mustard, Cadbury's foods, Mellow Birds coffee, Dunhill pipe tobacco, Guinness, and Bulmer's Cider.

Genealogy and Family History

As the interest in family history and roots grows world-wide, more and more people are turning to Frith's photographs of Great Britain for images of the towns, villages and streets where their ancestors lived; and, of course, photographs of the churches and chapels where their ancestors were christened, married and buried are an essential part of every genealogy tree and family album.

Frith Products

All Frith photographs are available Framed or just as Mounted Prints and Posters (size 23 x 16 inches). These may be ordered from the address below. From time to time other products - Address Books, Calendars, Table Mats, etc - are available.

The Internet

Already fifty thousand Frith photographs can be viewed and purchased on the internet through the Frith websites and a myriad of partner sites.

For more detailed information on Frith companies and products, look at these sites:

www.francisfrith.co.uk
www.francisfrith.com
(for North American visitors)

See the complete list of Frith Books at:
www.francisfrith.co.uk

This web site is regularly updated with the latest list of publications from the Frith Book Company. If you wish to buy books relating to another part of the country that your local bookshop does not stock, you may purchase on-line.

For further information, trade, or author enquiries please contact us at the address below:
The Francis Frith Collection, Frith's Barn, Teffont, Salisbury, Wiltshire, England SP3 5QP.
Tel: +44 (0)1722 716 376 Fax: +44 (0)1722 716 881   Email: sales@francisfrith.co.uk

See Frith books on the internet at www.francisfrith.co.uk

FREE MOUNTED PRINT

Mounted Print
Overall size 14 x 11 inches

Fill in and cut out this voucher and return
it with your remittance for £2.25 (to cover postage and handling). Offer valid for delivery to UK addresses only.

Choose any photograph included in this book.
Your SEPIA print will be A4 in size. It will be mounted in a cream mount with a burgundy rule line (overall size 14 x 11 inches).

**Order additional Mounted Prints
at HALF PRICE (only £7.49 each*)**
If you would like to order more Frith prints from this book, possibly as gifts for friends and family, you can buy them at half price (with no additional postage and handling costs).

Have your Mounted Prints framed
For an extra £14.95 per print* you can have your mounted print(s) framed in an elegant polished wood and gilt moulding, overall size 16 x 13 inches (no additional postage and handling required).

---

* IMPORTANT!

These special prices are only available if you order at the same time as you order your free mounted print. You must use the ORIGINAL VOUCHER on this page (no copies permitted). We can only despatch to one address.

Send completed Voucher form to:
The Francis Frith Collection, Frith's Barn, Teffont, Salisbury, Wiltshire SP3 5QP

Please do not photocopy this voucher. Only the original is valid, so please fill it in, cut it out and return it to us with your order.

Picture ref no	Page no	Qty	Mounted @ £7.49	Framed + £14.95	Total Cost
		1	Free of charge*	£	£
			£7.49	£	£
			£7.49	£	£
			£7.49	£	£
			£7.49	£	£
			£7.49	£	£

Please allow 28 days for delivery

* Post & handling (UK)	£2.25
Total Order Cost	**£**

Title of this book . . . .

I enclose a cheque/postal order for £ . . . .
made payable to 'The Francis Frith Collection'

OR please debit my Mastercard / Visa / Switch / Amex card
(credit cards please on all overseas orders), details below

Card Number

Issue No (Switch only)   Valid from (Amex/Switch)

Expires   Signature

Name Mr/Mrs/Ms . . . .

Address . . . .

. . . .

. . . .

. . . . Postcode . . . .

Daytime Tel No . . . .

Email . . . .

Valid to 31/12/05

Would you like to find out more about Francis Frith?

We have recently recruited some entertaining speakers who are happy to visit local groups, clubs and societies to give an illustrated talk documenting Frith's travels and photographs. If you are a member of such a group and are interested in hosting a presentation, we would love to hear from you.

Our speakers bring with them a small selection of our local town and county books, together with sample prints. They are happy to take orders. A small proportion of the order value is donated to the group who have hosted the presentation. The talks are therefore an excellent way of fundraising for small groups and societies.

Can you help us with information about any of the Frith photographs in this book?

We are gradually compiling an historical record for each of the photographs in the Frith archive. It is always fascinating to find out the names of the people shown in the pictures, as well as insights into the shops, buildings and other features depicted.

If you recognize anyone in the photographs in this book, or if you have information not already included in the author's caption, do let us know. We would love to hear from you, and will try to publish it in future books or articles.

Our production team

Frith books are produced by a small dedicated team at offices in the converted Grade II listed 18th-century barn at Teffont near Salisbury, illustrated above. Most have worked with the Frith Collection for many years. All have in common one quality: they have a passion for the Frith Collection. The team is constantly expanding, but currently includes:

Jason Buck, John Buck, Ruth Butler, Heather Crisp, David Davies, Isobel Hall, Julian Hight, Peter Horne, James Kinnear, Karen Kinnear, Tina Leary, Stuart Login, Amanda Lowe, David Marsh, Sue Molloy, Kate Rotondetto, Dean Scource, Eliza Sackett, Terence Sackett, Sandra Sampson, Adrian Sanders, Sandra Sanger, Julia Skinner, Claire Tarrier, Lewis Taylor, Shelley Tolcher and Lorraine Tuck.